Predator Attack!

By Katharine Kenah

School Specialty
Publishing

Columbus, Ohio

Library of Congress Cataloging-in-Publication Data

Kenah, Katharine.
    Predator attack!/by Katharine Kenah.
        p.cm.--(Extreme readers)
    ISBN 0-7696-3176-2 (pbk.)
    1. Predatory animals--Juvenile literature. 2. Animal attacks--Juvenile
literature. [1. Predatory animals. 2. Animal attacks.] I. Title. II. Series.

QL758.K46 2004
591.5'3--dc22
                                                      2003071097

 School Specialty.
Publishing

Send all inquiries to:
School Specialty Publishing
8720 Orion Place
Columbus, OH 43240-2111

ISBN 0-7696-3176-2

9 10 11 12 PHX 09 08 07 06

Have you ever seen a bear
with a shopping cart?
Wild animals must find
their own food in the wild.

Some animals catch and eat
other living things.
These animals are called *predators*.

Predators hunt to stay alive.
Food gives them energy to live.

Alligator

The alligator moves closer.
Snap! It swallows the turtle whole.

Alligators are fast.
They have lots of sharp teeth.
They use their teeth to attack.
They do not use their teeth to chew.

Weird Facts

- Alligators have brains the size of hot dogs.
- Clear third eyelids help alligators see underwater.

Bald Eagle

A bald eagle flies on the wind.
It spreads its huge wings.
Suddenly, the eagle drops from the sky.
It grabs a fish with its feet.

Eagles are good hunters.
Eagles can see farther and better
than any other animal!
Their long, sharp claws
are called *talons*.

Weird Facts

- Bald eagles are not bald. Their heads are covered with white feathers.

- The bald eagle is the national bird of the United States.

Barracuda

A barracuda is called
the "tiger of the sea."
It has long jaws and sharp teeth.
Watch out! It eats quickly!

Barracudas eat other fish.
They live in warm, tropical water
near coral reefs and sunken ships.

Weird Facts

- Barracudas can be poisonous if they eat smaller fish that have eaten poisonous marine plants.

- Barracudas can weigh over 100 pounds, about the weight of a very large dog.

Polar Bear

A polar bear is hunting on the ice.
Its thick fur keeps it warm.

Creamy white fur makes
polar bears hard to see.
When a seal pops up for air,
this polar bear will pounce on it!

Weird Facts

- Polar bears can smell food up to 10 miles away. They can sniff seal dens under 3 feet of ice and snow.

- Some polar bears weigh more than 1,000 pounds. This is about the weight of a horse.

Komodo Dragon

The world's biggest lizard
is looking for a meal. *Flick!*
It smells the air with its tongue.

Komodo dragons never get lost.
They follow smells on the ground
to find their way.
Their bites poison the blood
of their victims.

Weird Facts

- Komodo dragons have third eyes on the tops of their heads. These eyes sense light.
- Komodo dragons may have inspired mythical dragons. They both have long necks, lashing tongues and tails, and sharp teeth.

14

Gray Wolf

A gray wolf licks its lips.
It watches its prey, waiting to attack.
Gray wolves hunt sick or weak animals.

Gray wolves live in packs
with other wolves.
The wolves protect each other.
The howls of gray wolves can be
heard 10 miles away!

Weird Facts

- Wolves are part of the dog family. They are the largest wild dogs in the world.

- Ancient people may have learned how to hunt by watching wolves hunt in packs.

Tasmanian Devil

This Tasmanian devil is jumping,
trying to look big and mean.
Its pink ears turn deep red.
A Tasmanian devil does not want
to share food.

Tasmanian devils are marsupials.
They carry their babies in pouches.
Tasmanian devils sleep during the day.
They hunt at night.

Weird Facts

- Tasmanian devils' jaws and teeth are
  very strong. They can eat every bit of
  their prey. They can even eat the bones!

Spitting Cobra

This spitting cobra senses danger.
It rears back. Its neck flattens.
Now, the cobra is ready to spit
venom into its victim's eyes.

Cobra poison is strong.
Bites bring death within hours.
Baby cobras can bite as soon as
they hatch from their eggs.

Weird Facts

- One tablespoon of dried venom could kill 165 people.

- Spitting cobras can move forward with their heads raised and their bodies still coiled-up.

19

Cheetah

Whoosh! Is it a rocket or a race car?
No, it is a cheetah!
A cheetah is the world's fastest
mammal on land.

Cheetahs can leap 23 feet in one bound.
They can run at 70 miles per hour,
as fast as a car.
Cheetahs need to cool down in
the grass.

Weird Facts

- Cheetahs can go from 0 to 40 miles per hour in 2 seconds!

- Cheetahs' claws provide good traction because they do not retract. Their claws are always out.

Great White Shark

A great white shark
shoots through the water.
Its eyes roll back.
Its mouth opens wide, showing
seven rows of shiny white teeth.

Great white sharks are the
perfect killing machines.
They weigh more than most trucks.
They hear better than human beings.

Weird Facts

- Great white sharks are not all white. Their bodies are bluish-gray. Their bellies are white.

- Scientists believe these sharks have poor vision.

Brown Bear

A salmon swims *up* a waterfall. *Chomp!* It is caught by a large and powerful predator, the brown bear. The brown bear hunts with its strong jaws and huge paws.

Most animals walk on their toes.
Brown bears walk like people!
Each foot fully touches the ground
with each step.

Weird Facts

- Brown bears can run 25 miles per hour, as fast as an Olympic sprinter.
- Some brown bears weigh up to 1,700 pounds, as much as a car!

Badger

Do not let this sweet face fool you.
This short, furry creature
is a fierce fighter.
A badger has a pointed snout.
It hunts for food under leaves.

Badgers have long claws
for digging quickly!
They dig for food.
They also dig burrows to live in.

Weird Facts

- Snake venom only harms badgers if they are bitten on their noses.
- Badger fur is used to make paintbrushes.

Osprey

A fish wiggles to get away.
It is too late.
An osprey holds it in its claws.
The osprey's feet have tiny spikes.
The spikes help keep prey
from slipping away.

Ospreys build the biggest nests
of all the birds in North America.
They build them with sticks, seaweed,
and bones.
Some nests are 6 feet tall—
the size of a person!

Weird Facts

- Ospreys can plunge into water from high in the sky.

- Osprey nests can be seen for miles, perched atop trees, rocks, and poles.

Bengal Tiger

A Bengal tiger is the biggest
cat in the world.
It is very strong.
A Bengal tiger can live anywhere
that has food, shade, and water.

Bengal tigers can jump ten times
their length. They hunt at night.
Tiger stripes are like human fingerprints.
Every tiger has a different pattern.

Weird Facts

- Tigers' tongues are covered with spines for carrying water and combing the tigers' fur.

- Tigers attack from behind. Field workers wear masks of faces on the backs of their heads. This fools the tigers and prevents attacks.

EXTREME FACTS ABOUT PREDATORS!

- Alligators swallow stones to help them stay underwater.

- Eagles can see three to seven times farther than human beings!

- Over 1,000 barracudas can swim together. This big group of fish is called a *school*.

- Polar bears sometimes cover their black noses with their white paws, so seals will not see them.

- Komodo dragons can jog 6 miles without stopping.

- Wolves have a language of their own. It includes barks, woofs, and whimpers.

- If it is hungry enough, a Tasmanian devil will eat another Tasmanian devil.

- The king cobra can grow to over 18 feet long.

- Cheetahs run so quickly that at times all four feet are off the ground.

- Since they have no hands, sharks explore unfamiliar things with their teeth.

- Brown bears are shy creatures. They usually try to avoid fights.

- Badger fur was once used to line coats and jackets.

- Ospreys can have wingspans of over 6 feet.

- A tiger can eat 50 pounds of meat in one meal.